Meditations with Meister Eckhart

Including an analysis of

His Life and Times

Madonna Sophia Compton

Also by Madonna Sophia Compton:
Women Saints: 365 Daily Readings
Prayers of the Saints
Sophia-Spirit-Mary
Odes of Solomon (inclusive language)
Sisters in Wisdom
The Transcendent Feminine
More Glorious than the Seraphim

Meditations with the Saints (series)

Meditations with

Meister Eckhart

This book is dedicated to my
son, Shawn C. Hirsch

Meister Eckhart and the Emergence of Wisdom as Divine Ground

Historical Background

The vigorous expansion that was characteristic of European history from the early Middle Ages ended in the 1300s. It was a century when famine, plague and wars decimated populations. A recurrent archetypal theme in the consciousness of that era was the Four Horsemen of the Apocalypse. The Hundred Years War began in 1328 and did not end until 1453, during which time there was great peasant unrest and revolt.

Since the time of the Gregorian reforms of the 11th century the papacy had continued to build a Christian commonwealth which united Europe, following the great schism of 1054 which finally ended in the formal division of the Eastern and Western churches. Constantinople was captured, sacked and utterly demolished in the 4th crusade in 1204. In the late Middle Ages, the locus of power of the Roman Empire shifted into central Europe during the period of the Avignon papacy, (which included seven popes) most of which was marked by decadency. During this period the papacy was locked in a political contest with the French monarchy. Towns rebelled against local lords and bishops, crying out for charters of independence and self-government.

With popes, emperors and kings often feuding, the Holy Roman Empire was no longer a seamless garment; it was now divided into a temporal kingdom and a spiritual kingdom. In the past, when the papacy had faced criticism or crisis, reforming monastic orders had provided necessary spiritual cures, producing inspirational figures like Francis of Assisi, who started the Franciscan order, and the great scholastic Dominican, Thomas Aquinas. By the late 13th however, the Franciscans had become so worldly that a schism occurred with its ranks, (the Spiritual Franciscans wanting a simple return to poverty); and the Dominicans had become implicated with the Inquisition, a role which frequently led the laity to deeply distrust them. During this era, a new lay piety was emerging along the Rhine valley, where the famed Dominican Meister Eckhart was born (1260-1329) .

Eckhart may have studied under Albert the Great and was probably influenced by pseudo-Dionysius, the great Neoplatonist of the 6th century. He had a distinguished career as a prior provincial and preacher; indeed, he has often been called the most popular preacher in Germany. (1) As a preacher, Eckhart focused on four general areas: detachment, being formed again in God, the purity of the divine nature, and the nobility of the soul. Although his last years found him accused of heresy, he died within the bosom of the Church. The 14th century in Germany has often been referred to as the 'century of heresy' and was marked by a flowering of mysticism. This new mysticism was considered heretical because it was an intellectual resistance movement; in political terms, neither the empire, nor the Church and its sacraments, but the *soul*, was the Kingdom of God. Andrew Weeks has noted that "the violent and repressive aspects of public life, coupled with natural catastrophe made it appear plausible to interpret the mysticism of Eckhart as a turn inward in

the face of outer hardships and despair."
(2) Friedrich Heer sees in Eckhart an
amalgam of Stoicism, Origen, and the
Hellenic East. (3) His public preaching
was, however, always scriptural, and was
often given in convents. As Bernard
McGinn quotes the Meister, scripture
frequently tells a story "in such a way that it
also contains and suggests mysteries." (4)
These mysteries Eckhart took upon himself
to decipher.

Two years after his death, a number of
Eckhart's writings were condemned. Much
of his work, nonetheless, was absorbed
and disseminated by his disciples, the
foremost being John Tauler (1300-61) and
Henry Suso (1295-1366), who was
beatified. Among his readers and admirers
were Thomas à Kempis and Peter
Canisius. Although Eckhart relys on
classical Thomist scholastic dialectic, his
employment of an apophatic (or negative)
analysis often veers into what seems to be
an unorthodox pantheism. His teaching
spread to the Low Countries and as far as
England, represented in the classic *Cloud
of Unknowing*, and according to David
Knowles, two centuries later Tauler's
teaching had considerable influence upon

St. John of the Cross and Spanish mysticism. (5)

Influence and Teachings

Eckhart's writing has a surprising boldness of expression and an enduring power of mystical imagery. He was a major influence on German philosophy, from Hegel to Hiedegger. One finds the same Neoplatonic differentiation between God and Godhead, as is found in psuedo-Dionysius, who was a major figure in the apophatic mysticism in both East and West. Metaphysical concepts in Eckhart which seem to deviate from traditional scholastic canon were his notion of the 'fertility' of God, polarity between the Unmanifest and the Manifest Absolute, and the 'spiritual seed' or 'spark of the soul' which he identified as indestructible. These three themes are evident in the meditations that follow. Let us briefly examine his basic theory of Divine Wisdom to better understand his influence on disciples like Henry Suso and the whole of German mysticism.

The fertility of God arises from the overabundance of love which flows out, initially to the Son Logos and then to all of creation. Clearly, this has parallels with the Neoplatonic notion of 'overflow' of the One, (eg., in the cosmology of Plotinus) whose abundance of Being spills over into lower emanations. Eckhart says: "It is a miraculous thing that something flows out and yet remains within…" and "when the Father gave birth to all creatures he gave birth to me and I flowed out with all the creatures…" (6) The Incarnation forms a mid-point between the emanations in God and the production of creatures. God's speaking is God's creating. In the ideal ground of being which is the Word, God knows himself and this is also how we know God: "God's image is that he knows himself through and through…When the soul touches him with proper knowledge, it is like him in the image." (7)

Likewise, all created things "are called to return into whence they have flowed out." (8) In Sermon 25, we find this image of overflowing as it pertains to grace: "…first grace consists in a flowing out…from God; second grace [consists] in a flowing back…or return to God." (9) Through this overflow of God's *all,* everything in existence is held: "What God loves, that is something; but what God does not love, that is nothing, as the *Book of Wisdom* says." (10) Here Eckhart refers to Wisdom 11:25: "and how could a thing remain unless you willed it, or be preserved had it not been called forth by you?"

Eckhart distinguishes between the triune God and the hidden 'ground' or Godhead. His understanding of substance and relation in God, unlike Aquinas and nearly every other one of his predecessors, is legitimate only in thinking about God as three-who-are-one but in no way relates to the Unmanifest, hidden God. This hidden or divine darkness of the Godhead reveals the absolutely apophatic nature of his speculative mysticism. The soul is emptied of all images and metaphors in approaching the Godhead, including all representations of God in terms of time, place, body, and number.

Since God is beyond all definition, God is free to be "all in all." Eckhart says "God is free of all things, and therefore he *is* all things." (11) Because of God's radical freedom from any definition, there is nothing (including liturgical or scriptural, or anything using a verbal description) that can encompass the unutterable Deity, and if one has trouble understanding this, Eckhart seems to be saying, it is because one has not yet experienced it. Although phrases like "*is* all things" sounds pantheistic, Bernard McGinn tells us that understood correctly, it is not, for Eckhart continually wants to stress the total transcendence of God. "In response to objections to such passages brought up against him in the Cologne proceedings he invoked the distinction between the 'absolute existence' of God and the 'formally inherent existence' of creatures…" (12)

Besides the three faculties of the soul designated by Augustine—memory, intellect, and will—Eckhart postulates a 4th, which he calls a spark, or divine spark, which is created in the image of the transcendent Godhead. This sometimes seems to be incongruent with grace, and also hints of Origen's pre-existent soul. It was one of Eckhart's propositions that was condemned. Andrew Weeks explains that what Eckhart meant is that, "In regarding all things with equanimity, this power leaves place and time and self behind to become empty…Understood practically, the spark of the soul implies that those to whom he preached were capable of a divine knowledge, effected not by seeking, but by ceasing to seek." (13) What is reborn in the emptiness of the soul is the eternal Word of John 1:1. For Eckhart, the "birth of the Word in the soul [is] the breaking-through, or penetration of the soul into the divine ground that is the God beyond God." (14) This force or spark is the highest and most innermost part of the soul. In replying to his inquisitors, Eckhart presented the spark as created, but in the image of God. When all images have been expelled from the soul, the ground is made ready for this eternal birth. Eckhart's lofty, intuitive metaphysics here is aiming at the utter transformation of the individual, and a complete negating of egocentricity. For Eckhart, we fulfill our destiny when we affirm the existence of this spark; thus, we too are the 'Son'; and this same Logos informs the world by reflecting on itself through human self-knowledge.

Sophia or Divine Wisdom was, for Eckhart, most often identified with the Logos:

"It can be said that God's Wisdom, the Word, came into the world born according to the flesh in the middle of the night, following the text in Luke…"(Luke 2:8) (15) Since the Word is born in the individual when she or he experiences mystic union, this Biblical story is also an analogy for the soul: "Wisdom comes into the mind when the soul rests…when all things are silent to it and it is silent to all." (16) Eckhart said many times that the birth of the Son is an interior event, as can be seen in the following example:

"Everything which the Eternal Father teaches is his being, his nature and his total divinity. All this he reveals to us completely in his only begotten Son and teaches us that we are this same Son…God works all his works so that we might be the only begotten Son. When God sees that we are the only begotten Son, he is very quick to pursue us and acts as though his divine being were going to burst…so that he might reveal to us the utter abyss of his divinity and the fullness of his being and his nature." (17)

This passage captures the often repeated theme in Eckhart of the outpouring of love which is continually flowing into the Son— and through the Son to us— from this fertile God who cannot hold back his abundance of Being. (Rom 8: 32) However, Eckhart also treats Wisdom in a slightly different way, referring in particular to Wisdom 7: 27 ("And she who is One, can do all things.") Here Wisdom is related to the *ground* of Being, the Absolute One. This "One" is for Eckhart the highest perfection of God because "God is one which is indistinct." (18). All distinct things are two or more, but in Wisdom there occurs an indistinction pertaining to God's very nature; God is infinite and determined by nothing. Wisdom, since it is identified with the One, is here beyond other attributions of God, even the 'True' or the 'Good' and seems to coincide, for Eckhart, with the Monad of the Neoplatonists:

"The One which is called Monad, that is, unity, is not a number, but the source and origin of all number." Likewise: "God is indistinct and the Indistinct Itself." (19) Eckhart is so radical in his theology of God as unity that he parts company with Aquinas in his understanding of the Trinitarian relations, citing without disapproval the formula of Gilbert of Poitiers, (rejected by Thomas,) that the relations somehow remain *standing on the outside* of the divine substance.

This is because, for Eckhart, God's Substance alone is Ground (*Ungrund*). All else, in this very apophatic theology, emanates from this ground, and even though the Paternity is identified with the first Person of the Trinity, it is the Father and *not the Essence* that begets. Eckhart explains this by saying simply that "the difference between God and the Godhead is the difference between action and non-action." (20) Eckhart's path of negation is not unique; even in this somewhat extreme example it has a precedent in pseudo-Dionysius who said, "negations about God are true, but affirmations are unsuitable," as well as Maimonides, whom Eckhart knew very well. Maimonides, for example, held that negative propositions about the Creator are true, but affirmative propositions are partly equivocal.

Unity, for Eckhard has such an intimate association with Wisdom or Understanding, that at times, he seems to posit knowing as anterior even to being. In direct opposition to Aquinas, Eckhart asserts that God *does not know because he is*, but, rather he *is because he knows*. Gilson aptly notes that "however he may have expressed himself later on the subject of being, Eckhart never varied on this point: insofar as God is wisdom (sapientia) he is free of everything else, including being." (21) For Eckhart, the analogy is: what is it to understand another than to become one with what is understood?

Eckhart most frequently uses *esse, unum, or intelligere* as the transcendental divine ground of the hidden Godhead; whereas the Persons are most frequently identified as *ens, verum, and bonum. (22)* Gilson has noted that "one of the outstanding achievements of St. Augustine had precisely been to substitute the God of Exodus, that is, Being, for the "One" of Plotinus. This barrier seems to have finally given way, under the pressure of Proclus, in the doctrine of John Eckhart.... Eckhart knows very well that...he is running afoul of the text from Exodus (3:15)...but as the negative theology of Maimonides here reinforces the ontology of Proclus in an unexpected manner, he has the means of interpreting it." (23) Eckhart explains it thus:

"The still desert, into which no distinction ever crept—neither the Father, the Son, nor the Holy Spirit... This core is a simple stillness, which is unmoved itself but by whose immobility all things are moved and all receive life." (24)

Do we see in Wisdom, then, the 'First God' of the Platonists, that which in Kabbalah is known as the *Ain Soph*, i.e., the Unmanifest Absolute which alone is *One and the Source of all*? On the Jewish Tree of Life, which had been integrated into Christian Philosophy by the late Middle Ages, the first three Principles which emanate from Ain Soph are sometimes interpreted to constitute the first Kabbalistic Trinity.

If this is true, and it somehow *stands outside* of the Trinity, does the Trinity (as is the case in the Kabbalistic Tree of Life) somehow derive its source from this One? Or could this One somehow imply a 4th hypostasis? These are provocative questions which may, in fact, have led to the speculations drawn by some of Eckhart's inquisitors, but it appears that the paradoxical nature of the Meister's teaching most often eludes a cut-and-dried answer. In any event, sections of his work were not formally condemned until after his death and his principal students, Tauler and Suso, did their best to rehabilitate his teachings, thus ensuring their continued dissemination.

Eckhartian theology, it seems, strives to be non-dualistic, yet in doing so, poses new problems. To make detachment and emptiness rather than supernaturally infused love the agent for leading the soul to God risks the very real danger of self-deification, and indeed, this eventually emerged under the heresy of the 'Free Spirit,' which was characterized by a strong anti-clerical sentiment. For Eckhart, it emerges in his many apophatic statements, eg., he once said: "How, then, shall I love him? Love him as he is, a not-god, a not-spirit, apersonal, formless. Love him as he is the One, pure, sheer, limpid, in whom there is no duality..." (25) Here we see Eckhart speaking of God, not as Being, but as Nonbeing, or beyond being. The Russian theologian Sergius Bulgakov criticized Eckhart's mysticism as impersonal and soulless. (26). When the Transcendent God is imagined through the lens of radical theological apophaticism and considers it to be "more primordial" and "therefore metaphysically superior" to personal being, then it runs the risk of being "totally incompatible with the personalism of Christian philosophy." (27) Themes that imply a complete abnegation of the will such as we see in other radical apophatic mystics like Marguerite Porete, whose writings Eckhart himself is believed to have read, lead one to believe that the social gospel is not relevant. Indeed if we are called to love God as *non-spirit* and *a-personal* why then love or serve at all? Why not just *Be*? Most mystics need something 'personal' to love, and Eckhart's principle disciple, Henry Suso, finds its ultimate expression in the crucified Christ.

Themes which were developed by Eckhart's disciples or other medieval mystics, like Hildegaard or Mechthild, envision Wisdom as the Divine Bridegroom, who willingly enters into the suffering of humanity, or as the Wisdom figure who is the joyful partner of humans in the creative process (witnessed in the sapiential books). This vision of Wisdom, as developed by Bulgakov and other modern sophiologists, paint a portrait of Sophia who becomes the mediator and transformer of the mystic soul, but in a much more personal way. (28) Although Eckhart seems to define a Christ-Sophia who is the fount of Wisdom for the soul, he most often identifies with a cosmological Christ rather than with the historical Jesus.

Before we leave this brief excursion of the Meister's Understanding of Divine Wisdom, I would pose some additional questions for future research: what are the consequences of his radical theology of Sophia as Divine Ground? What are we to make of Eckhart's Abyss, which was his deepest understanding of God as Wisdom? For "abyss", as it continues to be used in the development of the sophiological tradition, has multiple meanings. Glenn Magee has noted that the German expression 'abgrund der Substanz' or the *Abyss of Substance,* first used in a philosophical context by Eckhart, seems to be the conceptual ancestor of Boehme's *ungrund*, or *ground,* which is the unmanifest, dark nature or "dark inchoate will for self-revelation." (29) Are there vestiges of gnosticism in Eckhart? If it is a small step from "Abgrund" to "ungrund", it is still a smaller one directly into the Abyss. And as Ioan Couliano dryly observes, if we read into Genesis a god who is demiurge, and who may, in fact, not know that above him, there is the *true God*, the result "is quite surprising, for it offers an explanation...of the fact that the Abyss, Darkness, and the Waters in Genesis do not seem to have been created by the Demiurge. If the Demiurge is only a second god, *then whatever is prior to him can be ascribed to the other* god." (30)

Despite the aspects of Eckhart's philosophy of God that may not represent the classical perceptions of dogmatic theology, Eckhart nonetheless was a great teacher in his day, and many of his mystical as well as practical words resound through history and remain a deep pool of Wisdom for us to ponder today.

Because he wrote many letters, including to the many women he counseled in convents and beguineges, there may be repetition in his sophianic themes, but for us, it helps to absorb his ideas expressed in a variety of different ways.

End Notes

1. In, *The Great German Mystics* by James Clark. NY: Russell and Russell, 1949, p. 9
2. Weeks, Andrew. *German Mysticism from Hildegard of Bingen to Ludwig Wittgenstein*. NY: State University of NY Press, 1993, p. 70.
3. Heer, Friedrich. *Intellectual History of Europe,* Vol. 1 Trans. by Jonathan Steinberg. N.Y.: Anchor Books, 1968 chap 10.
4. McGinn, *Meister Eckhart, the Essential Sermons, Commentaries, Treatises and Defense.* Trans. and Introduction by Edmund Colledge, O.S.A and Bernard McGinn, NY: Paulist Press. 1981. p 29.
5. Knowles, David. *The Evolution of Medieval Thought.* Helicon Press, Baltimore 1962, chapter 26.p. 314-15.
6. in *Deutsche Werke*,1,143, quoted in Weeks, *German...*1993, p. 79.
7. *Deutsche Werke* , 2,96 quoted in Weeks, p. 78.
8. McGinn, *Essential...*1981, page 30.
9. ibid.
10. McGinn, *Essential Sermons...*, p. 237.

11. *Deutsche Werke* 2, 497, quoted in Weeks, *German...* p. 83.
12. McGinn, *Essential*, p. 31.
13. Weeks, *German...*p. 81.
14. McGinn, *Essential*, p. 31.
15. Selections from Eckhart the Teacher, in *Meister Eckhart; Teacher and Preacher.* Ed. by Bernard McGinn NY: Paulist Press, 1986, p. 171.
16. ibid.,p. 171.
17. ibid, p. 267-8.
18. ibid, p. 166.
19. ibid, p. 167-8.
20. *Meister Eckhart; A Modern Translation* , Raymond Blackney, trans. NY: Harper & Row 1941, p. 225-6.
21. *History*, p. 439. Alternately, Gilson explains that, "Throughout his doctrinal career, he obstinately maintained that God the Father is Intellection, as he appropriated Life to the Son and Being to the Holy Spirit. By [this] solution, he put himself in conformity, as far as possible...with the Christian tradition."
22. *Essential Sermons*, p. 35.
23. *History...* pp. 438- 439.
24. Blackney, *Meister Eckhart*, p. 347.
25. *Meister Eckhart*, p. 248.
26. I have developed this theme in my *Sophia-Spirit-Mary: Sergius Bulgakov and the Patristric Roots of a Feminine*

Spirit. (2015) See also: Bulgakov, S. *The Comforter*, Wm. B. Eerdmans Publishing Co. 2004. pp. 44, 361.

27. ibid, p 361.
28. I have written about feminine mysticism in, Compton, Madonna Sophia: *Meditations with Hildegard of Bingen: Her Life and Times (2016); see also Meditations with Saints Gertrude and Mechthild, (2014)* ; and for Sergius Bulgakov, see #26, above.
29. In Magee, Glenn. *Alexander Hegel and the Hermetic Tradition*, Cornell University Press, 2001. p.38, p 163.
30. Couliano, Ioan. *The Tree of Gnosis: Gnostic Mythology from Early Christianity to Modern Nihilism.* Trans. By H.S Wiesner. SF: Harper. 1992, p. 134.

The Meditations

If the only prayer
You ever say in your entire life
 Is thank you,
It will be enough.

God is at home, it's we who have
gone out for a walk.

The price of inaction is far greater than the cost of making a mistake.

A human being has so many skins inside, covering the depths of the heart. We know so many things, but we don't know ourselves! Go into your own ground and learn to know yourself there.

We are celebrating the feast of the Eternal Birth which God the Father has borne and never ceases to bear in all eternity... But if it takes not place in you, what avails it? Everything lies in this, that it should take place in you.

God expects but one thing of you,
and that is that you should come out
of yourself in so far as you are a
created being, and let God be God in
you.

There exists only the present instant... a Now which always and without end is itself new. There is no yesterday nor any tomorrow, but only Now, as it was a thousand years ago and as it will be a thousand years hence.

You should perceive God
without an image,
without a medium,
and without comparisons.
And if you are to perceive God
in this way
without a medium,
He must become you.

Words derive their power from the original Word.

Compassion is where peace and justice kiss.

The eye with which I see God is the same eye with which God sees me.

The seed of God is in us. Given an intelligent and hard-working farmer, it will thrive and grow up to God, whose seed it is; and accordingly its fruits will be God-nature. Pear seeds grow into pear trees, nut seeds into nut trees, and God-seed into God.

The only thing that burns in hell is the part of you that won't let go of your life-- your memories, your attachments.

If you're frightened of dying and you're holding on, you'll see devils tearing your life away. They burn them all away, but they are not punishing you, they are freeing your soul.

If you've made your peace, then the devils are really angels freeing you from the earth.

The knower and the known are one.
Simple people imagine that they
should see God as if he stood there
and they here. This is not so. God
and I, we are one in wisdom.

You may go far or near but God
never goes far-off; he is always
standing close at hand, and even if
he cannot go within
He goes no further than the door.

You may call God love, you may call
God goodness. But the best name
for God is compassion.

We are all meant to be mothers of the Son of God. God is always needing to be born.

Every creature is a word of God.

If you would be serene and pure,
you need but one thing, detachment.

Whoever possesses God in their being, has him in a divine manner, and he shines out to them in all things; for them all things taste of God and in all things it is God's image that they see.

People should not worry as much about what they do but rather about what they are. If they and their ways are good, then their deeds are radiant. If you are righteous, then what you do will also be righteous. We should not think that holiness is based on what we do but rather on what we are, for it is not our works which sanctify us but we who sanctify our works.

There is a power in the soul which
touches neither time nor flesh,
flowing from the spirit, remaining
in the spirit, altogether spiritual.

It is a fair trade and an equal exchange: to the extent that you depart from things, thus far, no more and no less, God enters into you with all that is his, as far as you have stripped yourself of what is yours. It is here that you should begin, whatever the cost, for it is here that you will find true peace, and nowhere else.

The soul in which this birth is to take place must keep absolutely pure and must live in noble fashion, quite collected, and turned entirely inward: not running out through the five senses into the multiplicity of creatures, but all inturned and collected and in the purest part: there is His place; He disdains anything else.

The most important hour is always the present.
The most significant person is precisely the one sitting across from you right now.
The most necessary work is always love.

Theologians may quarrel, but the mystics of the world speak the same language.

If you love yourself, you love everybody else as you do yourself. As long as you love another person less than yourself, you will not succeed in loving yourself, but if you love all alike, including yourself, you will love them as one person and that person is both God and man. Thus he is the great righteous person who, loving himself, loves all others equally.

Though it may be called an ignorance, and unknowing, yet there is in it more than all knowing; for this unknowing lures and attracts you from all understood things, and from yourself as well.

The soul is scattered abroad among her powers, and dissipated in the action of each. Thus her ability to work inwardly is enfeebled, for a scattered power is imperfect.

The most powerful prayer, one well-nigh omnipotent, and the worthiest work of all is the outcome of a quiet mind. The quieter it is the more powerful, the worthier, the deeper, the more telling and more perfect the prayer is. To the quiet mind all things are possible. What is a quiet mind? A quiet mind is one which nothing weighs on, nothing worries, which, free from ties and from all self-seeking, is wholly merged into the will of God and dead to its own.

Do not imagine that your reason can grow to the knowledge of God.

Rather, be sure of this: absolute stillness for as long as possible is best of all for you.

Here God enters the soul with His all, not merely with a part: God enters here the ground of the soul.

You should know that God must act and pour Himself into the moment He finds you ready.

To be receptive to the highest truth, and to live therein, a person must be without before and after, untrammelled by all acts or by any images, empty and free, receiving the divine gift in the eternal Now, and bearing it back unhindered in the light of the same, with praise and thanksgiving in our Lord Jesus Christ.

That we may so truly remain within, that we may possess all truth, without medium and without distinction, in true blessedness, may God help us to do this.

Since it is God's nature not to be like anyone, we have to come to the state of being nothing in order to enter into the same nature that God is.

So, when I am able to establish myself in nothing, and nothing in myself, uprooting and casting out what is in me, then I can pass into the naked being of God, which is the naked being of the Spirit.

One means, without which I
cannot get to God, is work, that is:
activity in time which does not
interfere with eternal salvation.
'Works' are performed from
without, but 'activity' is practiced
with care and understanding
from within.

It is a certain and necessary truth that if you resign your will wholly to God, you will catch God and bind God, so that He can do nothing but what you most desire.

If you seek God and seek Him for your own profit and bliss, then in truth you are not seeking God.

We find people who like the taste of God in one way and not in another, and they want to have God only in one way of contemplation, not in another.

I declare truly that as long as anything is reflected in your mind which is not the eternal Word, or which looks away from the eternal Word, then, good as it may be, it is not the eternal thing.

For he alone is a good person who, having set at nought all created things, stands facing straight, with no side-glances, towards the eternal Word, for that soul is imaged and reflected there in righteousness.

There is a huge silence inside each of us that beckons us into itself, and the recovery of our own silence can begin to teach us the language of Heaven.

The human spirit must transcend number and break through multiplicity, so that God will break through; and just as He breaks through into me, so I break through into Him.

"In the beginning." Here we are given to understand that we are an offspring whom God has eternally borne out of the concealed darkness of the eternal concealment, remaining within, in the first beginning or the first purity, which is the plenitude.

Above thought is the intellect,
which still seeks: it goes about
looking, spies out here and there,
picks up and drops.

But above the intellect that seeks
is another Intellect which does not
seek but stays in its pure, simple
being, which is embraced in that
Light.

What does God do all day long?
He gives birth.
From the beginning of eternity
God lies on a maternity bed
giving birth to all.
God is creating this whole universe
full and entire
in this present moment.

Whoever possesses God in their
being has God in a divine manner,
Who then shines out to them
in all things; for to them
all things taste of God
and in all things it is
God's image that they see.

What is the last end? It is the hidden Darkness of the eternal divinity, and It is unknown, and it will never be known. God remains there within Himself, unknown, and the light of the Eternal Lord has eternally shone in There, and the darkness does not comprehend it. (Jn.1:5)

A person cannot flee from God.
Every corner where you go will
reveal God to you.
If you think you are fleeing God
you run into his lap.
Whether waking or sleeping
God bears his Only-Begotten Son
in you whether you like it
or not.

I often speak of a light that is
uncreated
and not capable of creation;
That always lives in the soul.
This same light comprehends God
without a medium, uncovered,
and naked, for you should know
this light is not content with
the divine nature's generative or
fruitful qualities.
For it wants to go into the simple
Ground, into the quiet desert,
into which distinction never gazed.

God is a word, a word
Unspoken.
But who can speak this word?
No one can do this except
Him who is the Word.
God is a Word that speaks itself.
The Father is a speaking word
and the Son is speech working.

The most powerful prayer
and almost the strongest of all to
obtain everything,
and the most honorable of all works
is that which proceeds from
an empty spirit.
The empty spirit can do anything.

An empty spirit is one that is
confused by nothing,
has not attached its best to any fixed
way of acting, and has no concern
whatever in anything
for its own gain.

Make a start with yourself
and abandon yourself truly.
If you do not begin by getting away
from yourself,
Wherever you run to, you will find
obstacles; the further you wander,
the less you find
what you are seeking.

The will is complete and just
when it is without any self-seeking
and when it has forsaken itself.
And in that will
You can accomplish anything.

But you must know
that God's friends are never
without consolation, for whatever
God wills is for them the greatest
consolation of all, whether it be
consolation or desolation.

The more we possess ourselves
the less do we possess.
A person who has gone out of what
is his own could never fail to find
God in anything he did.

Many of his works
Christ performed with the intention
that we should imitate him
spiritually not physically.
And so we ought to do our best
to be able to imitate him
with our understanding, for
He values our love
more than our works.

In truth, all that we lack
is true faith.
We may think that what we see or
feel benefits us more than faith,
But that is only because we
obey external rules.

The sufferings of the senses
and of the inferior powers
and the opposition they meet
is not the spirit's concern;
For the greater and more violent
the conflict is, the greater
and more praiseworthy
is the victory and the glory.

Even if one does not
have longing for God
one should prepare for it
and act as if one had it
and act as it requires,
For to become holy here
in time
is to follow God.
And that is eternity.

Grace does not destroy nature.
It perfects it.
Glory does not destroy grace,
It perfects it.
So we should not destroy in
ourselves any good thing,
however small it may be,
Even for the sake of something
great.
Rather, we should bring it
to its greatest perfection.

If we can find God
always,
everywhere,
with everyone
and in every way,
we can always go on
increasing
and growing,
and never come to the end
of our increasing.

The one who has God
essentially present to oneself
grasps God divinely. Then God
shines in you in all things. And
everything tastes to you of God and
God will form himself for you out of
all things.
In this way, God always shines out in
you.

Printed in Great Britain
by Amazon